Zebras

By Sally Cowan

Zebras are animals
that live in Africa.

Zebras walk across the land
in herds.

They look for plants to eat.

Zebras need to drink a lot
to stay alive in the heat.

They look around for pools
to drink from.

Zebras look like horses, apart from their coats!

A zebra has black and white marks along its body and legs.

Zebras may all look alike to us,
but each zebra's marks
are a bit different.

Big cats, such as cheetahs, hunt zebras.

A zebra's marks can help it hide from cheetahs.

Zebras are most safe
when they are not alone.

All their marks get mixed up.

The cheetah can not see
which zebra to attack!

Zebras can stand up
when they are asleep.

They rest on each
other's backs.

A few zebras in the herd
stay awake.

If a zebra sees a cheetah,
it yips like a dog!

The sleeping zebras wake up
and run away.

But if a cheetah attacks, zebras can fight back!

They stand and kick **hard**.

The cheetah runs away.

It knows that a kick could break its bones!

A zebra foal can stand up as soon as it's born.

It has long legs to run along with the herd.

We can see zebras in the wild or at a zoo.

Zebras are amazing animals!

CHECKING FOR MEANING

1. What do zebras eat? *(Literal)*

2. What is the weather like where zebras live? *(Literal)*

3. Why would a cheetah want to attack a zebra? *(Inferential)*

EXTENDING VOCABULARY

zebras	*Zebras* means more than one zebra, and *zebra* is the singular form. What other words in the text mean more than one of something? E.g. animals, plants, horses, pools, legs.
alike	What does *alike* mean? What other words do you know that have a similar meaning? E.g. same, similar. What is the opposite to *alike*?
awake and asleep	What do these words mean? Do they have a similar meaning or the opposite meaning? Which word in the text has a similar meaning to *sleep*?

MOVING BEYOND THE TEXT

1. Discuss with students the meaning of the word *camouflage.* Explain that camouflage helps to keep animals safe in the wild. Find other pictures to show how different animals can be camouflaged.

2. Each zebra has a different pattern of stripes. Talk to students about the unique pattern of lines that make up their fingerprints.

3. A baby zebra is called a foal. Discuss the names given to other baby animals that students are familiar with.

4. Talk about how and why the zebra enclosure at a zoo is made to look like where zebras live in the wild.

THE SCHWA

a   e   i   o   u

PRACTICE WORDS

animals

Africa

across

zebras

alive

around

the

a

apart

along

different

cheetahs

alike

alone

asleep

away

zebra

awake

amazing

zebra's

A

The

cheetah

Zebras

attack

attacks